HAL•LEONARD

Jazz Play-Along

Book and CD for B♭, E♭, C and Bass Clef Instruments

volume 99

Swinging Standards

10 FAVORITE TUNES

Arranged and Produced by Mark Taylor and Jim Roberts

ISBN 978-1-4234-6386-3

HAL•LEONARD® CORPORATION
7777 W. BLUEMOUND RD. P.O. BOX 13819 MILWAUKEE, WI 53213

Visit Hal Leonard Online at
www.halleonard.com

SWINGING STANDARDS

Volume 99

Arranged and Produced by
Mark Taylor and Jim Roberts

Featured Players:

Graham Breedlove–Trumpet
John Desalme–Saxes
Tony Nalker–Piano
Jim Roberts–Bass
Joe McCarthy–Drums

Recorded at Bias Studios, Springfield, Virginia
Bob Dawson, Engineer

HOW TO USE THE CD:

Each song has two tracks:

1) Split Track/Melody

Woodwind, Brass, Keyboard, and **Mallet Players** can use this track as a learning tool for melody style and inflection.

Bass Players can learn and perform with this track – remove the recorded bass track by turning down the volume on the LEFT channel.

Keyboard and **Guitar Players** can learn and perform with this track – remove the recorded piano part by turning down the volume on the RIGHT channel.

2) Full Stereo Track

Soloists or **Groups** can learn and perform with this accompaniment track with the RHYTHM SECTION only.

AIN'T THAT A KICK IN THE HEAD

WORDS BY SAMMY CAHN
MUSIC BY JAMES VAN HEUSEN

C VERSION

5

ALL OR NOTHING AT ALL

WORDS BY JACK LAWRENCE
MUSIC BY ARTHUR ALTMAN

C VERSION

AS LONG AS I LIVE

LYRIC BY TED KOEHLER
MUSIC BY HAROLD ARLEN

C VERSION

BUT SHE'S MY BUDDY'S CHICK

EAST OF THE SUN
(AND WEST OF THE MOON)

WORDS AND MUSIC BY
BROOKS BOWMAN

C VERSION

I THOUGHT ABOUT YOU

WORDS BY JOHNNY MERCER
MUSIC BY JIMMY VAN HEUSEN

CD
🎵 : SPLIT TRACK/MELODY
🎵 : FULL STEREO TRACK

C VERSION

LET THERE BE LOVE

LYRIC BY IAN GRANT
MUSIC BY LIONEL RAND

17

THE MAN THAT GOT AWAY

FROM THE MOTION PICTURE A STAR IS BORN

LYRIC BY IRA GERSHWIN
MUSIC BY HAROLD ARLEN

CD
◆ **19** : SPLIT TRACK/MELODY
◆ **20** : FULL STEREO TRACK

C VERSION

19

PENNIES FROM HEAVEN

FROM PENNIES FROM HEAVEN

WORDS BY JOHN BURKE
MUSIC BY ARTHUR JOHNSTON

C VERSION

LOVE IS A SIMPLE THING

WORDS BY JUNE CARROLL
MUSIC BY ARTHUR SIEGEL

C VERSION

LOVE IS A SIMPLE THING

CD
- 15 : SPLIT TRACK/MELODY
- 16 : FULL STEREO TRACK

WORDS BY JUNE CARROLL
MUSIC BY ARTHUR SIEGEL

Bb VERSION

AIN'T THAT A KICK IN THE HEAD

WORDS BY SAMMY CAHN
MUSIC BY JAMES VAN HEUSEN

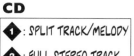

25

ALL OR NOTHING AT ALL

CD
3: SPLIT TRACK/MELODY
4: FULL STEREO TRACK

WORDS BY JACK LAWRENCE
MUSIC BY ARTHUR ALTMAN

Bb VERSION

CD

◆ 5 : SPLIT TRACK/MELODY
◆ 6 : FULL STEREO TRACK

AS LONG AS I LIVE

LYRIC BY TED KOEHLER
MUSIC BY HAROLD ARLEN

Bb VERSION

BUT SHE'S MY BUDDY'S CHICK

WORDS AND MUSIC BY SY OLIVER
AND CHARLES S. ATKINSON

EAST OF THE SUN
(AND WEST OF THE MOON)

WORDS AND MUSIC BY
BROOKS BOWMAN

CD
◆ 9 : SPLIT TRACK/MELODY
◇ 10 : FULL STEREO TRACK

Bb VERSION

I Thought About You

WORDS BY JOHNNY MERCER
MUSIC BY JIMMY VAN HEUSEN

Bb VERSION

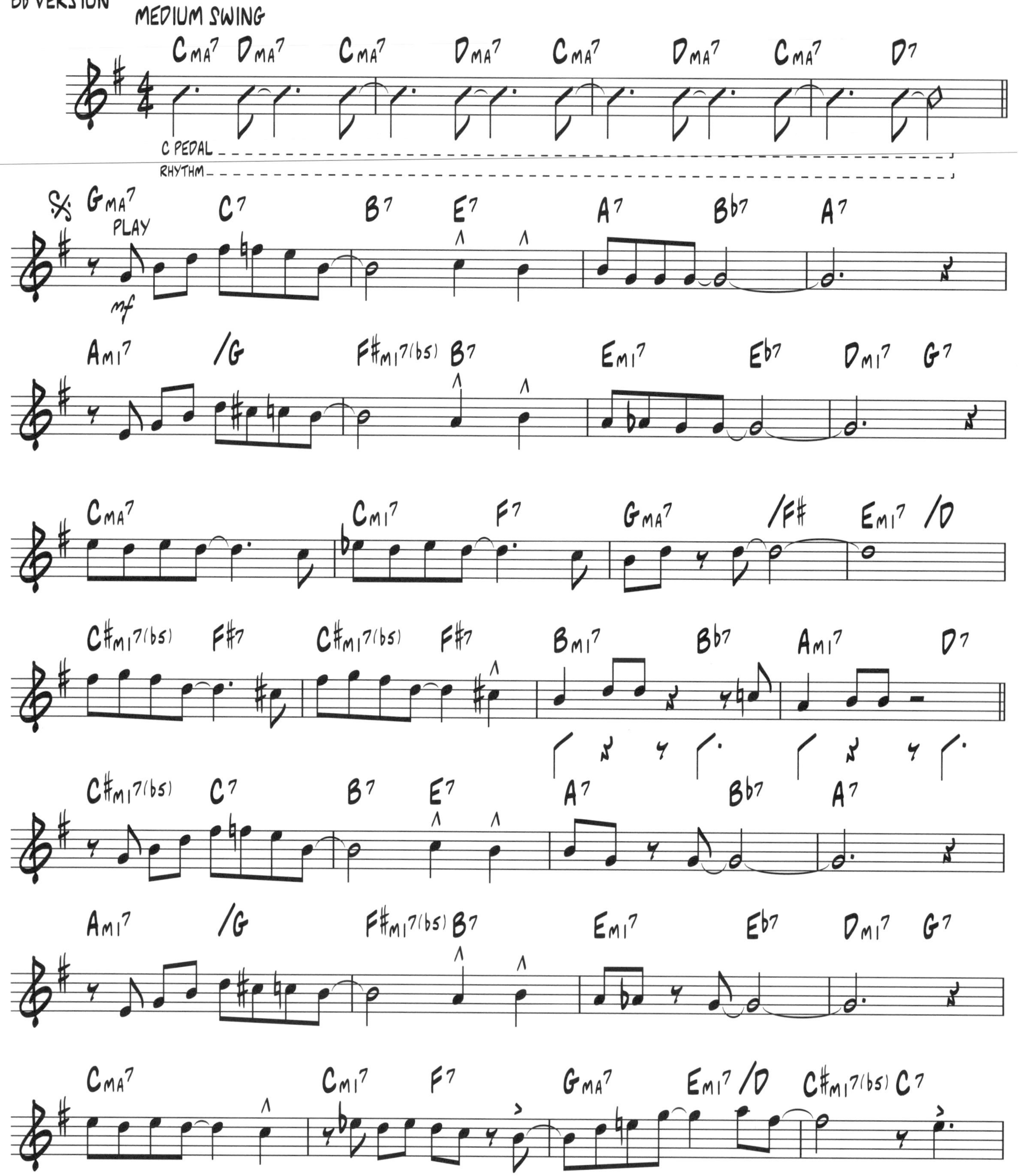

MEDIUM SWING

LET THERE BE LOVE

LYRIC BY IAN GRANT
MUSIC BY LIONEL RAND

Bb VERSION

37

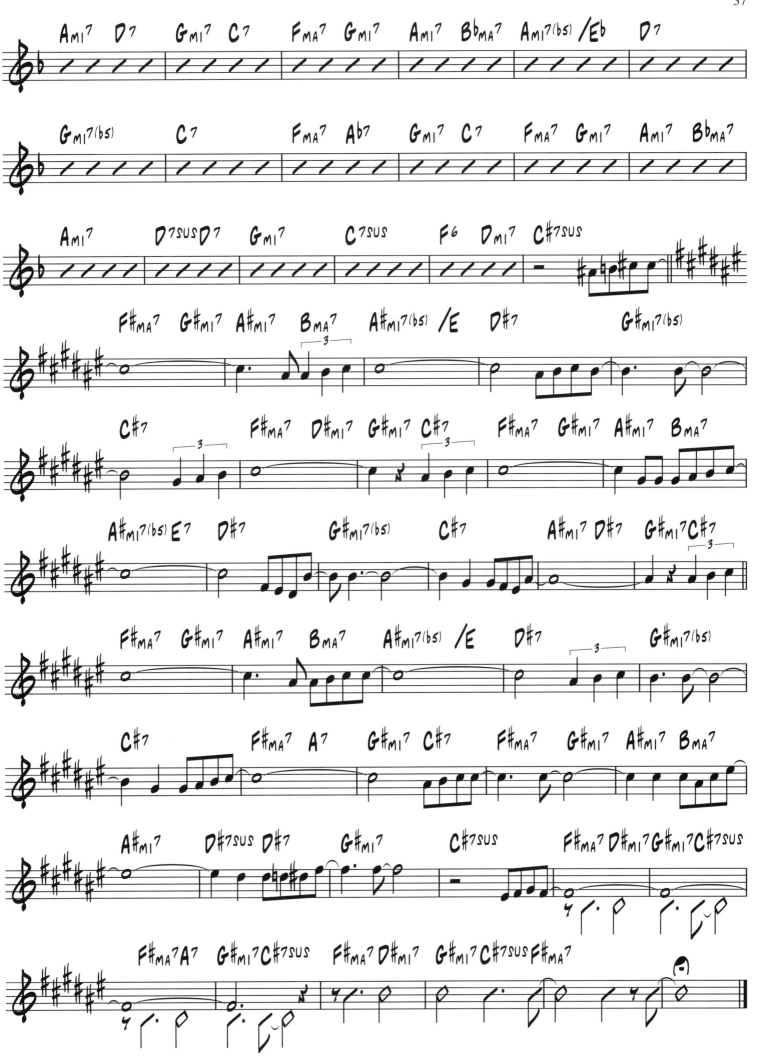

THE MAN THAT GOT AWAY

FROM THE MOTION PICTURE A STAR IS BORN

LYRIC BY IRA GERSHWIN
MUSIC BY HAROLD ARLEN

CD
19 : SPLIT TRACK/MELODY
20 : FULL STEREO TRACK

Bb VERSION

CD

17 : SPLIT TRACK/MELODY
18 : FULL STEREO TRACK

PENNIES FROM HEAVEN

FROM PENNIES FROM HEAVEN

WORDS BY JOHN BURKE
MUSIC BY ARTHUR JOHNSTON

Bb VERSION

41

AIN'T THAT A KICK IN THE HEAD

WORDS BY SAMMY CAHN
MUSIC BY JAMES VAN HEUSEN

Eb VERSION

All or Nothing at All

WORDS BY JACK LAWRENCE
MUSIC BY ARTHUR ALTMAN

Eb Version

AS LONG AS I LIVE

LYRIC BY TED KOEHLER
MUSIC BY HAROLD ARLEN

Eb VERSION

EAST OF THE SUN
(AND WEST OF THE MOON)

WORDS AND MUSIC BY
BROOKS BOWMAN

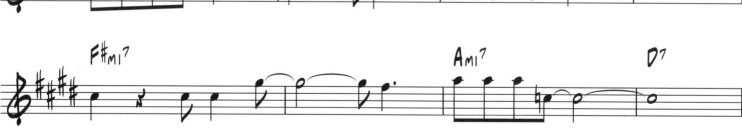

I Thought About You

WORDS BY JOHNNY MERCER
MUSIC BY JIMMY VAN HEUSEN

CD
🎵 : SPLIT TRACK/MELODY
🎵 : FULL STEREO TRACK

Eb VERSION

53

Let There Be Love

CD

19 : SPLIT TRACK/MELODY
20 : FULL STEREO TRACK

THE MAN THAT GOT AWAY

FROM THE MOTION PICTURE A STAR IS BORN

LYRIC BY IRA GERSHWIN
MUSIC BY HAROLD ARLEN

Eb VERSION

57

CD

17 : SPLIT TRACK/MELODY
18 : FULL STEREO TRACK

PENNIES FROM HEAVEN

FROM PENNIES FROM HEAVEN

WORDS BY JOHN BURKE
MUSIC BY ARTHUR JOHNSTON

Eb VERSION

LOVE IS A SIMPLE THING

WORDS BY JUNE CARROLL
MUSIC BY ARTHUR SIEGEL

LOVE IS A SIMPLE THING

WORDS BY JUNE CARROLL
MUSIC BY ARTHUR SIEGEL

AIN'T THAT A KICK IN THE HEAD

WORDS BY SAMMY CAHN
MUSIC BY JAMES VAN HEUSEN

63

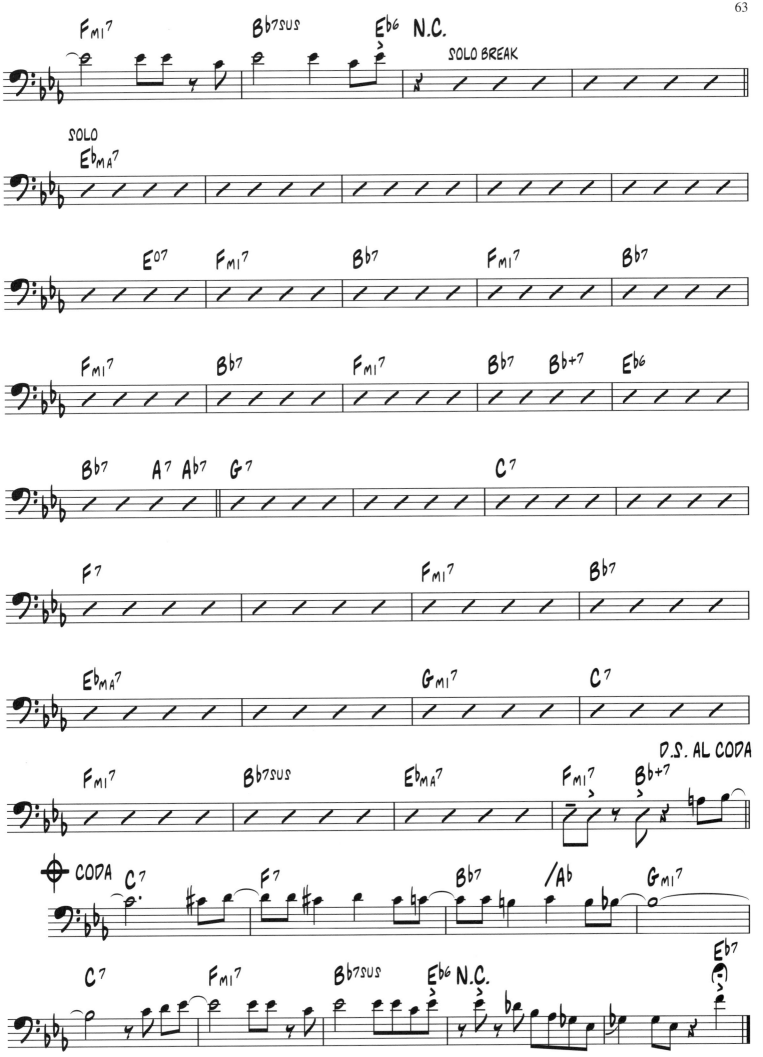

ALL OR NOTHING AT ALL

WORDS BY JACK LAWRENCE
MUSIC BY ARTHUR ALTMAN

𝄢: C VERSION

As Long As I Live

LYRIC BY TED KOEHLER
MUSIC BY HAROLD ARLEN

𝄢 : C VERSION

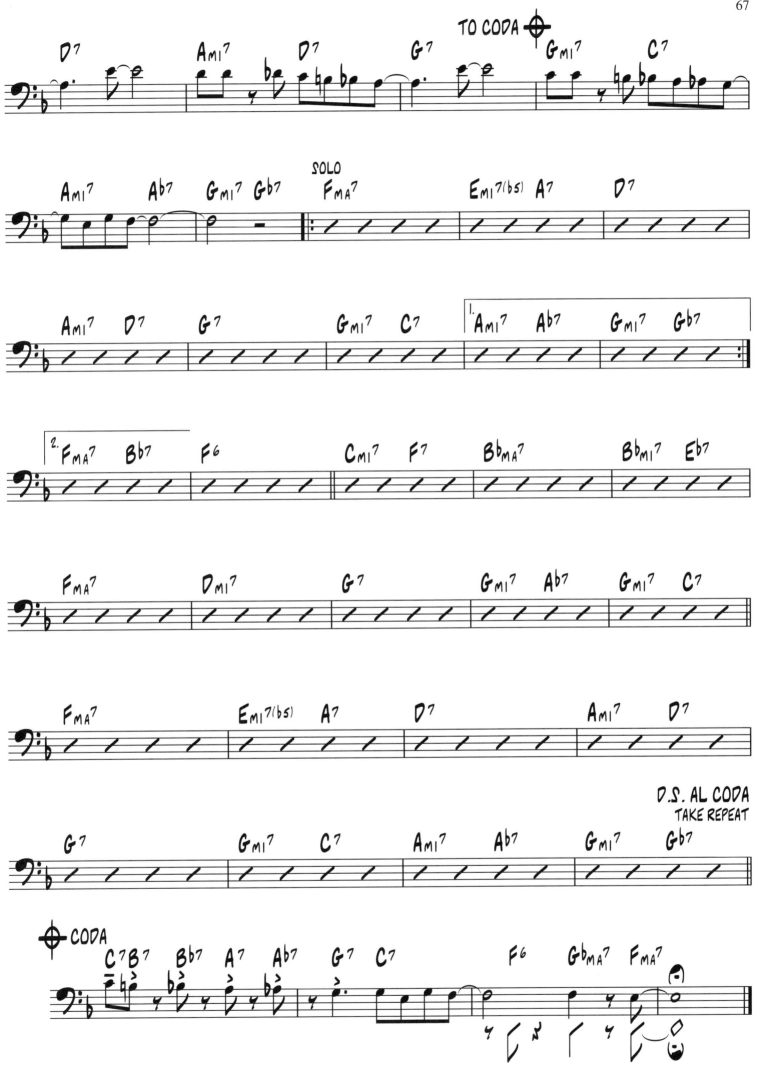

BUT SHE'S MY BUDDY'S CHICK

WORDS AND MUSIC BY SY OLIVER
AND CHARLES S. ATKINSON

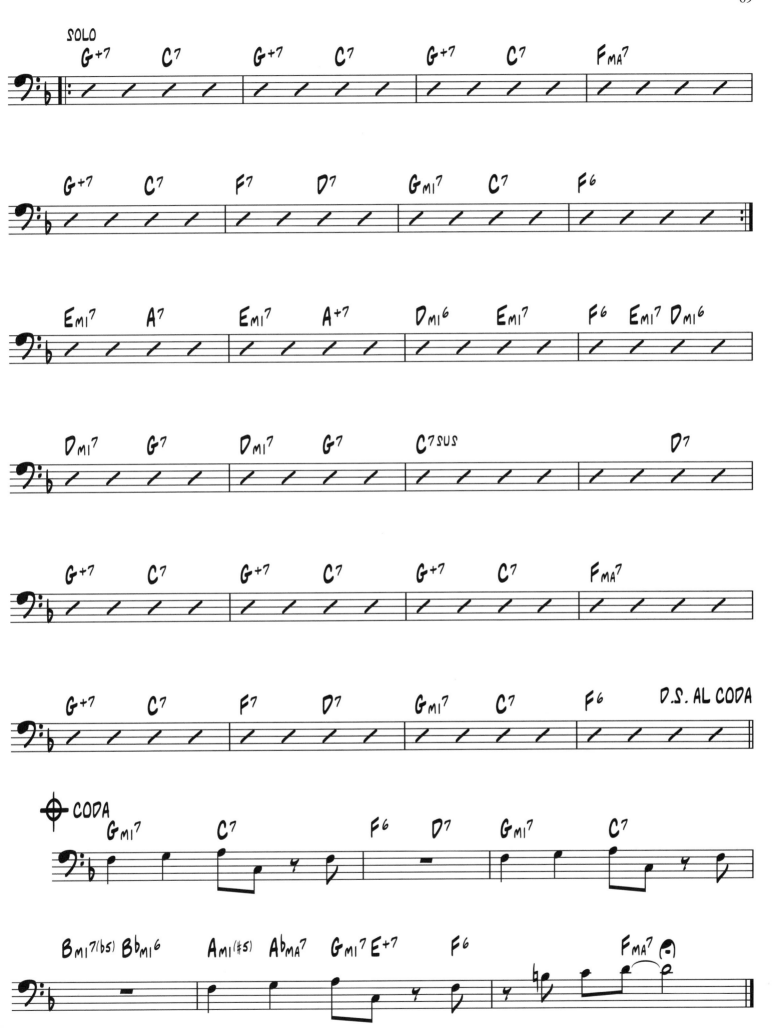

CD
- 9 : SPLIT TRACK/MELODY
- 10 : FULL STEREO TRACK

EAST OF THE SUN
(AND WEST OF THE MOON)

WORDS AND MUSIC BY
BROOKS BOWMAN

𝄢: C VERSION

I Thought About You

WORDS BY JOHNNY MERCER
MUSIC BY JIMMY VAN HEUSEN

CD
- 11: SPLIT TRACK/MELODY
- 12: FULL STEREO TRACK

𝄢: C VERSION
MEDIUM SWING

Let There Be Love

LYRIC BY IAN GRANT
MUSIC BY LIONEL RAND

75

CD

THE MAN THAT GOT AWAY
FROM THE MOTION PICTURE A STAR IS BORN

LYRIC BY IRA GERSHWIN
MUSIC BY HAROLD ARLEN

C VERSION

PENNIES FROM HEAVEN

FROM PENNIES FROM HEAVEN

WORDS BY JOHN BURKE
MUSIC BY ARTHUR JOHNSTON

𝄢: C VERSION

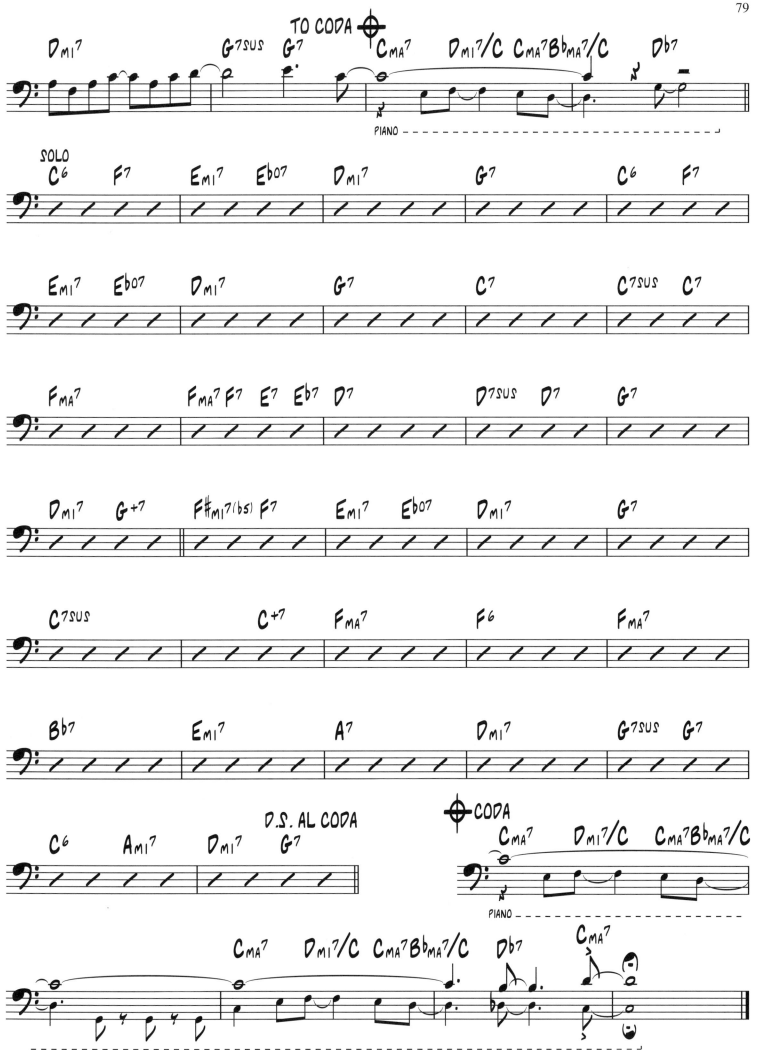